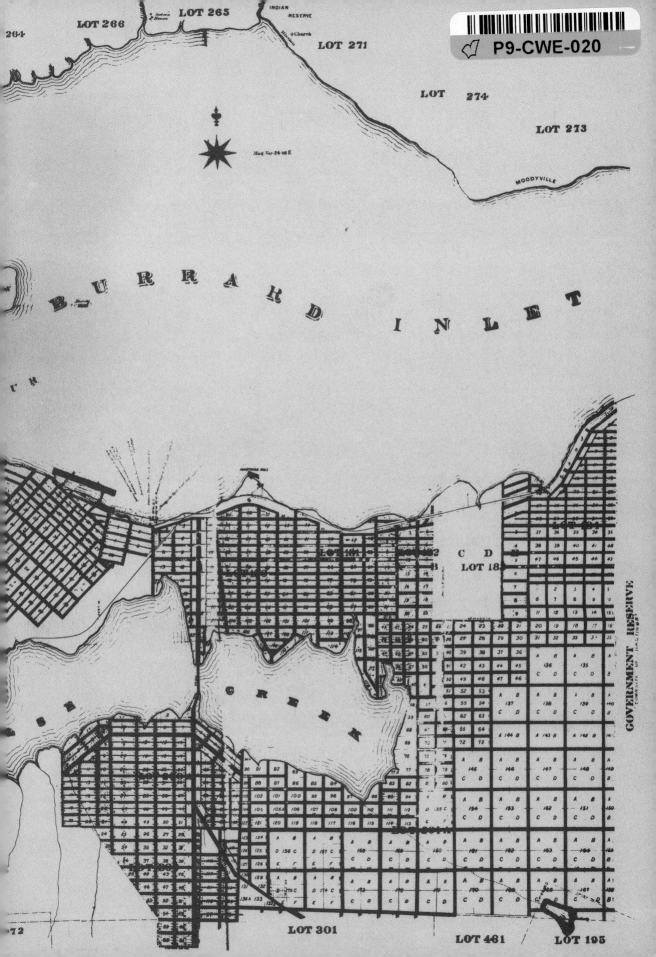

Vancouver's Past

Raymond Hull
Gordon Soules
Christine Soules

Published by GORDON SOULES ECONOMIC AND MARKETING RESEARCH
355 Burrard Street, Vancouver, Canada, V6C 2G8
British Address: 2 Cockspur Street, London, England SWIY 5BQ
Also published in the United States by the University of Washington Press

Acknowledgements

We would like to thank the many people who assisted us in our research for this book, especially: Ron D'Altroy and his staff of the Photographic section, Aileen Tufts and her staff of the Business and Economics section, and Elizabeth Walker and her staff, of the Northwest History section of the downtown Vancouver Public Library; R. Lynn Ogden and his staff, of the Vancouver Archives; Anne Yandle and her staff, of the Special Collections division of the University of B.C. Library; and Dr. Warren L. Cook, Professor of History and Anthropology, Castleton State College, and author of *Flood Tide Of Empire,* who provided valuable information on the early explorers of this coast.

We also thank these people for invaluable help during the final stages of the work, in reading the manuscript, advising on the selection of photographs, etc.: Dr. Charles E. Borden, Professor Emeritus of Archaeology at the University of B.C.; Ron D'Altroy, Photographic Curator of the Vancouver Public Library; Margaret Ginther, Library Co-ordinator, Vancouver School Board; Norman Hacking, marine historian and Vancouver newspaper columnist; Dr. Walter Hardwick, Vancouver Alderman and Professor of Geography at the University of B.C.; Barbara Howard, teacher, Southlands Elementary School, Vancouver; O. F. Landauer, Leonard Frank Photos; Joseph Lawrence, Assistant Professor, Department of History, University of B.C.; Len McCann of the Vancouver Maritime Museum; R. Lynn Ogden, archivist, Vancouver Archives; Lynn Prosser, teacher, Charles Dickens Elementary School, Vancouver; Harvie L. Walker, Project Manager, Canadian Studies Project, Vancouver School Board; and Robert Watt, president of Vancouver Historical Association and curator of history, Vancouver Centennial Museum.

We also express our appreciation of Dr. A. L. Lazenby's valuable work in compiling the index.

Sources of Photographs and Maps

Vancouver Public Library, 21, 26, 29 bottom, 35 top, 36, 39, 47 bottom, 48, 53, 55, 56, 58 top, 58 bottom, 59, 62 bottom, 67, 69, 73 top, 73 bottom, 74/75, 76, 78, 81, 82 top, 82 bottom, 83, 84.
Vancouver Archives, inside front and back cover, 4, 15, 16, 35 bottom, 37, 38, 40/41, 45, 49 bottom, 62 top, 68, 72, 77.
Provincial Archives, Victoria, B.C., 7, 24/25, 25 bottom, 28/29, 32/33, 63, 64.
Helmut Hirnschall, 6, 22/23, 79, 90/91.
Notman Photographic Archives, McCord Museum, Montreal, Quebec, 42, 43, 51.
Woodward Stores Ltd., 54, 60/61, 86.
City of Victoria Archives, 46/47, 46 bottom.
The University of B.C., 12, 71.
George Allen Aerial Photos Ltd., 65, 87.
Frank Grundig, front cover.
Vancouver Maritime Museum, 44.
Provincial Museum, Victoria, B.C., 9.
National Harbours Board, 92.
National Portrait Gallery, London, England, 14.
B.C. Department of Lands, Forests and Water Resources, 27.
B.C. Hydro and Power Authority, 49 top.

First Printing June, 1974   25,000 Copies

International Standard Book Number: 0-919574-02-5
Library of Congress Catalog Card Number: 74-77919

Published by GORDON SOULES ECONOMIC AND MARKETING RESEARCH
355 Burrard Street, Vancouver, Canada, V6C 2G8
British Address: 2 Cockspur Street, London, England SWIY 5BQ
Also published in the United States by the University of Washington Press

CONTENTS

PHOTOGRAPHY   *Front cover by Frank Grundig.*
CARTOGRAPHY   *Helmut Hirnschall*
BOOK DESIGN   *George Crawford*
TYPESETTING   *Vancouver Typesetting Co. Ltd.*
PRINTED IN CANADA *Smith Grant Mann Ltd.*
PUBLISHER   *Gordon Soules Economic and
                   Marketing Research*
Also published in the United States by the University of Washington Press.

*Squamish Indian, August Jack Khahtsahlano; born about 1877
at Snauq, died 1967.*

4

1

Early Indian Settlement

Two hundred years ago, the area now occupied by Greater Vancouver was covered with a dense forest of fir, spruce, hemlock and cedar. About 5,000 Indian people lived in villages near the water's edge. The present-day place-names Musqueam and Squamish derive from native groups who had their main villages at those sites.

These Musqueam and Squamish people spoke different languages from the Indians farther up and down the coast, yet they were loosely connected by intermarriage and by a broad similarity of culture.

Musqueam is on the north bank of the North Arm of the Fraser River, in the southwest corner of Vancouver. The Musqueam people also had settlements farther up the Fraser, and on Burrard Inlet.

The main Squamish villages stood on the river-banks at the head of Howe Sound. There were other Squamish settlements farther south on Howe Sound, and in Burrard Inlet.

Indian Place-Names

Homulcheson village stood on the east bank of Homulcheson Creek, now Capilano River. Eyalmox was at the west end of Jericho Beach. Snauq was on the south shore of False Creek, just east of the Centennial Museum and Planetarium.

Whoi-Whoi, meaning "Masks", was on the site of Lumbermen's Arch in Stanley Park; there Indian ceremonial masks were made. Ayyulshun, meaning "Soft under feet", is now English Bay bathing beach. Checheyohee, "The Twins", were the peaks now called The

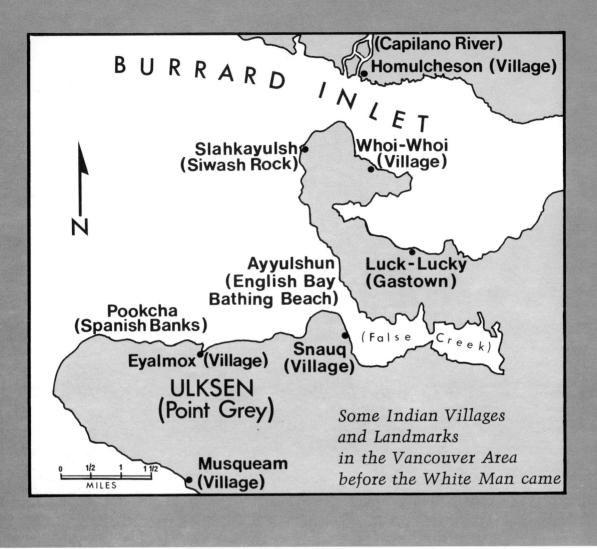

Some Indian Villages
and Landmarks
in the Vancouver Area
before the White Man came

Lions. Slahkayulsh, "He is standing up", is now called Siwash Rock. ("Siwash", a corruption of the French "Sauvage", is a name considered offensive by many of the native people.)

Social Organization

Many people today think that all Indians belonged to "tribes", ruled by hereditary or elected "chiefs". In this area there were no "tribes" and no "chiefs". What the white man called a "tribe" was simply a number of people, residing near each other, who spoke the same language. Several related families — the men might be brothers, cousins or brothers-in-law — lived in one big building. This multiple household was the basic social unit. Several such households formed a village.

Each household had its own leader and conducted its own affairs without control by any "chief". If a problem required joint action, the

6

Indian huts of split cedar, Stanley Park, 1868. Six dugout canoes in foreground.

household heads would meet and decide what to do. In an emergency involving two or more villages — a war, for example — one man might be elected leader for that specific occasion. When it was over, he would generally return to his former position; however, if he were a clever leader, he might retain his new status.

Order and property-rights were maintained largely by social pressure; anyone who misbehaved would be scorned as "low class".

Dwelling Places

For the Indian, land was not divided into lots, each owned by one person. People did not have fixed residences: a family might live at two, three or more different places in the course of a year.

During the cool, rainy winter months, the Musqueam and Squamish lived in long-houses, mostly of similar design. The single-pitch roof, sloping from front to back, was supported by a post-and-beam framework and covered with long, wide cedar boards. The walls were of horizontal cedar planks, lashed to a double set of upright poles, one inside, the other out. There were usually two doorways, in the end walls, near the front corners of the house.

One house might be several hundred feet long, divided by partitions into single-family apartments, each about forty feet square. Fires were built on the earth floor, and some of the roof-boards could be pushed aside by poles to let out the smoke. Against the walls were sleeping-platforms of wood or earth. The residents sat, and slept, on rush mats.

A village consisted of a single row of long-houses, always close to a river or the sea, for easy access to the cedar dugout canoes that were the sole means of travel and transportation.

In spring, summer and fall, many of the people were away from these villages, hunting, clam-digging, harvesting fruits, herbs, edible roots and seaweeds, catching, drying and smoking fish, dressing hides, or trading with Indians from other areas.

Many families had exclusive hereditary sites for certain purposes, such as dip-netting salmon, trapping sturgeon and digging camas bulbs, to which they went year after year. There, some had permanent drying-racks and houses; others built temporary lean-to shelters. These hereditary locations might be miles from the winter village. For example, August Jack Khahtsahlano, from whose family name is derived the place-name Kitsilano, told Major J. S. Matthews, the former Vancouver Archivist, that Snauq was a Squamish village, but that some Musqueams had seasonal fishing rights on the nearby sandbar which later became Granville Island.

Food Supply
The people of this area had plenty of meat — bear, deer, beaver and elk — which was either eaten fresh, or preserved by being cut into strips and dried.

Salmon, sturgeon, halibut, flounder and trout were dried or smoked. The oolichan was pressed for oil, or dried. Crabs and clams were taken from the beaches.

The women picked wild berries, dried them and pressed them into 3-pound blocks; or berries were put in a sack and immersed in the cold water of a creek, where they kept fresh for a long time. Women also dug roots with sharp sticks. Some were dried whole; others, such as fern roots, were ground to powder for storage.

8

Carved human figure post, said to have been set up by the second Capilano to commemorate his father, a famous warrior; photographed at Musqueam, 1898.

Clothing

In fine weather, the women wore knee-length wrap-around skirts of woven cedar-bark fibre; some men wore fringed breech-clouts; some went naked. In rainy weather, men and women wore capes of animal skin, woven dog or goat hair, or bark fibre. Some had broad-brimmed rain-hats of bark or root fibre. Summer and winter, they generally went barefooted.

They wore no elaborate feathered head-dresses. Some men used a narrow head-band to control their hair, and then might stick a single feather into the band. They used sharp stones to cut their hair to a little less than shoulder-length.

Arts and Crafts

The Squamish and Musqueam used plant fibres, wood, stone, shell, bone and gem-stones to make baskets, boxes, dishes, spoons, knives, jewelry, masks, musical instruments, tobacco-pipes and canoes. Many of the articles were elaborately carved or painted with stylized motifs from their heraldry and legends — animals, birds, fishes, ancestral heroes or spirit-beings. Totem poles were used by some Indians farther up the coast, but not by the Squamish and Musqueam.

Leisure

In this bountiful environment, the people did not have to work all year round; they had ample leisure time, and enjoyed many games and sports.

Boys rolled a wooden ball along the ground, and shot at it with bows and arrows.

The men competed in canoe racing, wrestling, tug-of-war, and in a kind of field-hockey with six-man teams, wooden clubs and a stone ball.

There was much gambling by individuals and by teams, using crescent-shaped dice of beaver teeth or short gambling-sticks incised with lines and dots.

Particularly important were the winter festivals. These were full of story-telling, dance-drama and pantomime, with music, singing, and elaborately-costumed actors. Some such performances were public, held by firelight in a long-house with the partitions removed. Some were private, for the initiates of the various secret societies.

The potlatch was a ceremony at which one household entertained guests with oratory, dancing, singing and feasting, and presented them with gifts such as blankets, weapons, canoes and slaves. A big potlatch might attract several hundred guests, many from far away, and might last for weeks. To prepare for it, the host family would work and save for months or years; the more lavish the hospitality, the greater was the status they acquired in the community.

Yet it was understood that the guests were obliged to return this hospitality at a later date. The hosts' expense was therefore an investment that would yield a handsome return, and the potlatch was a system of social insurance as well as a festive occasion.

2

Early European Exploration

Much of the early European exploration on this coast was in search of a Northwest Passage, a sea-route joining the Atlantic and Pacific coasts.

Explorers were also seeking fish, furs, minerals and other resources, sites for harbours, trading posts and colonial settlements, and waterways that would give access to the continental interior. Some of them traded with the Indian people, exchanging European clothes, knives, beads and pieces of metal for seal, bear and sea-otter skins, fish, Chilkat blankets and finely-sewn buckskin garments. In all these activities there was considerable international rivalry, notably among Spain, Britain and Russia.

Some of the claims by European explorers, including Juan de Fuca and Vitus Bering, concerning who discovered this coast, have been disputed; nevertheless, the archives of Spain and Spanish America still contain much unexamined material that may confirm or disprove their reports. Our present information suggests that the first European to sight what is now British Columbia was Juan Pérez, Captain of the *Santiago*, who discovered the Queen Charlotte Islands and anchored at the entrance of Nootka Sound in 1774.

The first Europeans to land there were Captain James Cook and his companions, in 1778. His men traded iron, copper and trinkets for sea-otter skins which they later sold very profitably in China. Within a few years, British and American traders were briskly competing for the coastline's peltry.

To fend off these challengers to Madrid's claims, in 1789 the Spanish built a fort at Nootka Sound and claimed possession. After some dispute, the Nootka Convention of 1790 left ownership of the region unsettled, but gave equal trading rights to Britain and Spain. In this period of empire building, the rights of the Indians to the land were generally ignored.

In 1790, Manuel Quimper sailed from Nootka and explored the Strait of Juan de Fuca, and in the summer of 1791 two small Spanish naval vessels were sent to press on further.

Narváez

Lieutenant José María Narváez (pronounced Nar-va-eth) in the schooner *Santa Saturnina* and second pilot José Verdia in a longboat passed through Rosario Strait, east of what are now called the San Juan Islands, then headed northwest, mapping as they went such parts of the coastline as they could see. Shoals and adverse winds often forced them offshore; fog and rain sometimes hid the land.

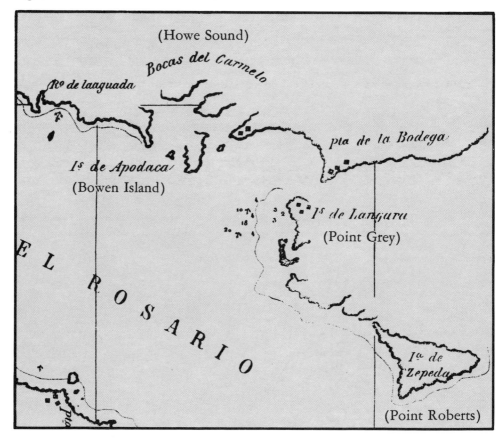

Part of a Spanish map in the Depósito Hydrográfico, Madrid, showing Narváez's discoveries in this area in 1791. Present-day names of some features have been added in brackets.

12

They passed Boundary Bay and Point Roberts, saw to starboard the low-lying islands at the mouth of the Fraser River, and on July 5 anchored west of a 250-foot headland, later called Point Grey; they took it for part of another island group, which they named Islas de Lángara.

From their village on the headland, some Musqueam paddled out to the schooner and traded meat, vegetables, water and firewood for sheets of copper and pieces of iron.

Narváez's log-books are lost, but a surviving Spanish map, based upon his discoveries, shows several Indian villages around Burrard Inlet.

Narváez next examined the entrance to Howe Sound, Bocas del Carmelo, then sailed on up the coast.

(Narvaez Drive, in Vancouver, was named after him in 1941. Langara Golf Course, at 49th Avenue and Cambie Street, took its name from Narváez's supposed islands.)

Vancouver

In 1792, Captain George Vancouver came around the Cape of Good Hope and through the Indian Ocean to the Pacific, with orders from the British Admiralty to explore the coast from 30°N, 200 miles south of the present United States-Mexican border, to 60°N, near the present Seward, Alaska. He was to report on settlements made by other European nations; he was to go to Nootka and take possession, from the Spanish, of lands and buildings; and, with a view to finding the Northwest Passage, he had particular instructions to explore every major inlet to its headwaters.

Vancouver left his two sailing vessels, *Discovery* and *Chatham*, anchored in Birch Bay, just south of the Canada-United States border, to make astronomical observations and check the chronometers. In the yawl of the *Discovery*, accompanied by Lieutenant Peter Puget in the launch, Vancouver sailed and rowed northwest along the coast.

He determined the latitude and longitude of Point Grey, then sailed into the inlet, passed north of Stanley Park, under the 200-foot bluff at Prospect Point, and into First Narrows.

Vancouver wrote in his journal: "Here we were met by about fifty Indians, in their canoes, who conducted themselves with great decorum, and civility, presenting us with several fish cooked...These good people finding we were inclined to make some return for their hospitality, showed much understanding in preferring iron to copper."

The boats proceeded into the broader part of the harbour. Vancouver described the future site of the city: "The shores...on the southern side, of a moderate height, and though rocky, well covered with trees

Portrait of an unknown man, once thought to be Captain George Vancouver. Recent research by the National Portrait Gallery, in London, England, revealed that this is not Vancouver.

Captain Vancouver's two sailing vessels, Discovery and Chatham, from a painting by F. P. Thursby.

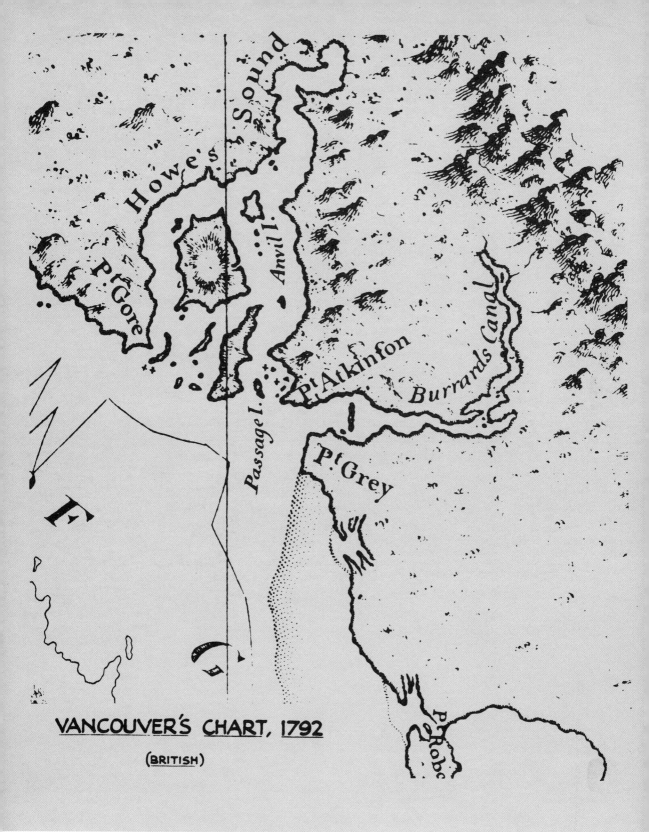

Part of Captain Vancouver's chart. The mouths of the Fraser are shown as two bays; Stanley Park is shown as an island.

16

of large growth, principally of the pine tribe."

The date was June 12, 1792. Vancouver's report says the 13th, but he had not allowed for the day lost in crossing the 180th meridian.

Vancouver named the inlet Burrard's Canal, after a naval friend, Sir Harry Burrard. He sailed on to a point within sight of the head of the inlet where his men tried in vain to catch fish with a net. The Indians, seeing their failure, promised to give them fish the next day.

Vancouver wrote: "A great desire was manifested by these people to imitate our actions, expecially in the firing of a musket, which one of them performed, though with much fear and trembling. They minutely attended to all our transactions, and examined the colour of our skins with infinite curiosity."

Vancouver's party spent the night there, near present-day Port Moody. At 4 a.m. they sailed again. They saw, but did not explore, the entrance to Indian Arm, and passed through Second Narrows, the main harbour, and First Narrows. Few of the Indians were up; two canoes put out from the beach at First Narrows, but could not catch Vancouver's boats, which now had a fresh, favourable wind. By 7 a.m. the Englishmen were off Point Atkinson, named by Vancouver after another naval friend. They explored Howe Sound and Jervis Inlet, and then turned south to rejoin their ships.

Galiano and Valdés

On June 21, off Point Grey, Vancouver saw two vessels at anchor, flying the colours of the Spanish Navy. They were the *Sutil,* commanded by Dionisio Alcalá Galiano and the schooner *Mexicana* under Caye-tano Valdés.

Vancouver, Lieutenant Puget and a midshipman boarded the *Sutil.* "Senor Galiano, who spoke a little English, informed me, that they ... had sailed ... to complete the examination of this inlet, which had, in the preceding year, been partly surveyed by some Spanish officers ..."

The Spaniards produced Narváez's chart; Vancouver showed them his; and they cordially agreed to co-operate in further exploration of the coast. Vancouver says: "Their conduct was replete with that polite-ness and friendship which characterizes the Spanish nation ... having partaken with them a very hearty breakfast [I] bad them farewell ..."

Vancouver's party had a hard day's rowing against unfavourable winds to get back to Birch Bay and the ships.

On June 23, Vancouver sailed up the coast and rejoined the Spaniards, who had meanwhile explored Indian Arm. They gave him a copy of their chart of it.

Thus were mapped the west and north portions of the site of Vancouver;

no European had yet visited the southern portion, along the Fraser River.

Fraser

The first white explorer to see the south side of the peninsula was Simon Fraser, a partner in the North West Company, a fur trading company competing with the Hudson's Bay Company.

The North West Company's posts in what is now the northern interior of British Columbia were being expensively and inefficiently supplied from Montreal. Fraser hoped to find a better supply route from the west coast. In May, 1808, he and twenty-three men left Fort George, now Prince George, to seek the mouth of the south-flowing river that he believed to be the Columbia. (The river was eventually named after him, the Fraser.)

Near Pavilion, rocks and rapids forced him to abandon his four canoes and continue on foot. The terrible hardships of the 150-mile portage convinced Fraser that this could never be a major trade route; yet he persevered, and finally brought his men out alive at the foot of the canyon, to the place later called Yale.

Borrowing dugout canoes from the natives there, he paddled westward, toward the sea. He was warned that the coastal Indians were at war with the up-river people, and would probably be hostile to anyone coming downstream. But he pushed on, past the sites we know as New Westminster, Burnaby and Marpole, to the river mouth. There, astronomical observations showed him that the latitude was approximately 49°N. But he knew that the latitude of the Columbia's mouth was about 46°N. This was the wrong river!

On July 2, he landed at the village of Musqueam. On his approach, most of the inhabitants withdrew into the woods, leaving behind only a few old people, one of whom showed Fraser and his crew around their houses. Fraser later wrote in his journal that, as they were leaving, "The natives ... began to make their appearance from every direction, in their coats of mail, howling like so many wolves, and brandishing their war clubs."

One of Fraser's assistants, Jules Quesnel, later wrote in a letter to a friend at Montreal: "... it was the greatest good luck that we were able to escape from this awkward situation without being obliged to kill and to be killed ourselves."

So, without actually entering the Strait of Georgia, Fraser turned east for the five-week struggle upstream to Fort George.

See the monument to Fraser's landing at Musqueam, on South West Marine Drive, one and one-half miles west of Camosun Street.

18

3
Early White Settlement

There was no rush of settlers on the heels of the explorers. Thirty-six years passed after Narváez mapped Islas de Lángara, nineteen years passed after Fraser landed at Musqueam, before any white people came to live in the Lower Mainland. Nootka, on Vancouver Island, had been abandoned since 1795.

Fur Trading

In 1821, the Hudson's Bay and North West Companies amalgamated under the Hudson's Bay Company's name; shortly afterwards the company set up its western headquarters at Fort Vancouver, ninety miles up the Columbia River, now Vancouver, Washington. Increasing numbers of American settlers and traders moved into the area, and American trading ships plied far up the northwest coast.

The Hudson's Bay Company saw that, to meet this competition, they would have to set up more trading posts; so in 1827 they founded Fort Langley, thirty miles from the mouth of the Fraser River. Here the Indians brought furs to trade for steel hatchets, knives, files and needles, muzzle-loading guns, powder, lead and bullet-moulds, Lucifer matches, hardtack, tobacco, yard goods, buttons and the heavy Hudson's Bay blankets.

In 1843, the Hudson's Bay Company founded Fort Camosun, later called Fort Victoria, at the southern tip of Vancouver Island.

In 1846, the Oregon Treaty set the mainland boundary between American and British territory along the 49th parallel, with Britain keeping all Vancouver Island. The mainland of what is now British Columbia was at this time known as New Caledonia. Three years later, the Company transferred its western headquarters from Fort Vancouver to Fort Victoria. In the same year, Vancouver Island became a British crown colony and the Company gained control of the Island by promising to bring out colonists. However, in practice, throughout its territory, the Company discouraged settlers who would clear the forest and drive away the fur-bearing animals that were the basis of its trade.

Gold Rush!

The gold rush of 1858-59 brought 25,000 men to the banks and sand-bars of the Fraser. Most of them came from California, where the gold rush was declining, up-coast to Victoria or Port Angeles, and across to the Fraser by steamers, canoes, rafts or homemade boats.

Victoria and Fort Langley turned from quiet little settlements into bustling boom-towns. In 1858,the British Parliament created the colony of British Columbia on the mainland, and James Douglas was sworn in at Fort Langley as its governor. The following year, New Westminster became the colony's capital, the centre of its trade and administration, and its chief port.

An Alternative Port

British naval authorities knew that New Westminster might any winter be closed by ice. Seeking a nearby salt-water anchorage for their war-ships, they chose the head of Burrard Inlet, now Port Moody. In 1859, the Royal Engineers built the North Road from New Westminster over the hills to this harbour.

The winter of 1861-62 showed the wisdom of this decision; for three months the Fraser was frozen to its mouth and steamers had to go into Burrard Inlet. Mails and passengers were hauled from Port Moody to New Westminster by sleigh.

Vancouver Ignored

The future site of Vancouver up to this time had attracted no white settlers. The land contained no gold, and there seemed nothing else to coax men away from the Fraser.

Coal and Clay

In 1862, three young Englishmen, returning to New Westminster after unsuccessfully prospecting in the interior, determined to cash in on the local shortage of building materials. John Morton, William Hail-stone and Samuel Brighouse pre-empted 550 acres of land adjoining Burrard Inlet. They were mocked as "The Three Greenhorns" for going to such an out-of-the-way place; but their land contained a coal seam

Oxen pulling logs down a skid road near the present site of the Marine Building at Burrard and Hastings Streets, 1882.

and a bed of clay, and Morton, who came from a well-known family of English potters, recognized its value.

Just west of the present site of the Marine Building, at the north foot of Burrard Street, they built a cabin, a small barn and a kiln, and began to make bricks. This "Brickmakers' Claim" comprised what is now the entire West End of Vancouver! The Greenhorns are generally recognized as the first white settlers on the site of the city.

Farming

About the same time, several farms were established near the Fraser River. One or two of these farmers may have been in business even before the Three Greenhorns went to Burrard Inlet. Yet this southern section of the Burrard Peninsula was for many years outside the city limits, so the farmers, rightly or wrongly, are not generally thought of as the first white settlers of Vancouver.

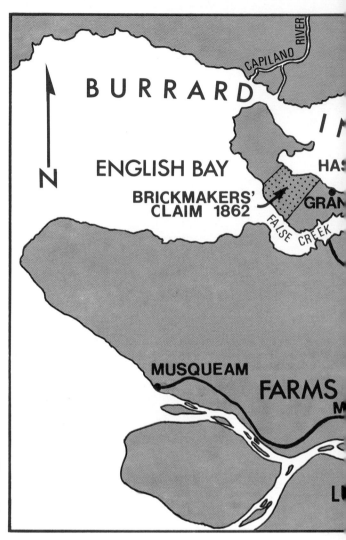

*Early Settlements
and Trails
in the Vancouver Area
prior to 1871*

Lumber

Logging first brought settlers in substantial numbers to the site of present-day Vancouver. English Bay and Burrard Inlet had some of the finest stands of easily accessible timber in the world.

In 1863, Pioneer Mills began operation on the North Shore, about half a mile east of present-day Lonsdale Avenue, North Vancouver. The first cargo of lumber went to New Westminster on August 12, aboard the woodburning sternwheel steamboat *Flying Dutchman*. The major markets for Burrard Inlet lumber at this time were New Westminster, Nanaimo and Victoria. On November 9 the following year, the sailing ship *Ellen Lewis* sailed with a cargo of lumber for Australia — the first export of goods from Burrard Inlet to a foreign country.

In 1865, Captain Edward Stamp built a sawmill on the South Shore,

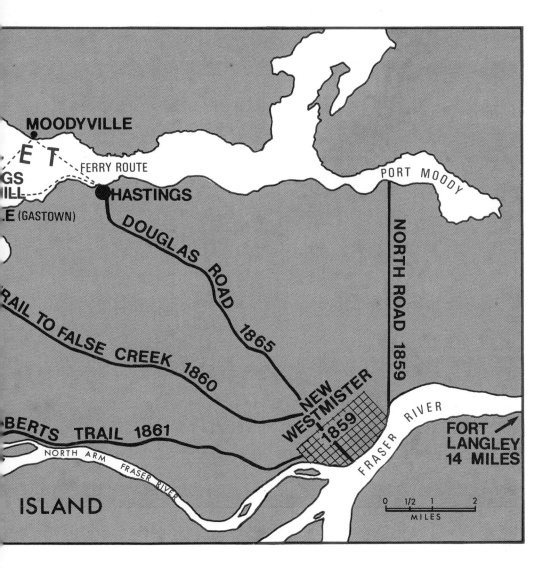

MOODYVILLE

ET

GS
ILL

FERRY ROUTE

E (GASTOWN)

HASTINGS

DOUGLAS ROAD 1865

RAIL TO FALSE CREEK 1860

BERTS TRAIL 1861

NORTH ARM FRASER RIVER

ISLAND

PORT MOODY

NORTH ROAD 1859

NEW WESTMISTER 1859

FRASER RIVER

FORT LANGLEY 14 MILES

0 1/2 1   2
MILES

near the foot of Dunlevy Avenue, but delays in getting machinery from Britain kept the mill idle for two years. Meanwhile Stamp exported hand-hewn ships' spars. When the mill finally got going in 1867, its steam-powered saws could cut 30,000 feet of lumber a day. Teams of oxen hauled logs out of the woods along skid roads — greased wooden skids laid several feet apart.

Now at Burrard Inlet, in good times, several hundred loggers and shake-cutters were at work. The mills hired many Musqueam and Squamish Indians; some of them moved their families, and built new villages on Burrard Inlet, to be near their work.

By the late sixties there was a thriving export trade with Australia, San Francisco and South America. The lumber was loaded in sailing ships, which were usually towed into and out of the Inlet by local steam

23

Hastings Mill (formerly known as Stamp's Mill) as seen from Granville, 1872.

tugs; but some shipmasters, to save the cost of a tow, would wait for a favourable wind and tide, then sail through First Narrows — no mean feat of seamanship, since the navigable channel was much narrower and shallower than it is now.

Two Teetotal Towns

Among the stumps of the clearing around Stamp's Mill on the South Shore sprang up a little shacktown for the mill-hands and supervisors. There was a wharf for small boats and a store that sold food, clothes, cooking pots and patent medicines, but no liquor. *See the Old Hastings Mill Store at Point Grey Road and Alma Street.*

Moodyville, the town which had grown around the mill on the North Shore, named after mill-owner Sewell Prescott Moody, was also strictly teetotal.

Loggers, mill-workers and ships' crewmen, if they wanted a drink, had to hike the 20-mile round-trip to New Westminster, over the newly opened Douglas Road that reached Burrard Inlet near the present Pacific National Exhibition grounds.

"Gassy Jack" Deighton

The economic potential of satisfying several hundred thirsty wage-earners attracted John "Gassy Jack" Deighton, a hotel-keeper and former steamboat pilot from New Westminster. In 1867, he built a saloon just west of Stamp's property-line. (The site is the middle of the present five-way intersection in Gastown.)

John Deighton,
"Gassy Jack", 1830-1875.

Beside his saloon sprang up a village known, after its first citizen, as Gastown. By March, 1870, its six blocks had been surveyed and officially named Granville Townsite.

Gassy Jack is considered Vancouver's founding father. The city's street-numbering system starts from the site of his saloon.

Social Life at the Inlet

North Road, from New Westminster to the head of the Inlet, was soon abandoned; Douglas Road became the main overland link with New Westminster. At the north end of Douglas Road, Oliver Hocking and Fred Houston built a hotel to cater to Inlet residents and to serve as a pleasure resort for the young people of New Westminster, who came by stage in summer, by sleigh in winter.

Water Street in the 1870s. On the extreme left are guests on the verandah of Deighton House, Gassy Jack's hotel and saloon.

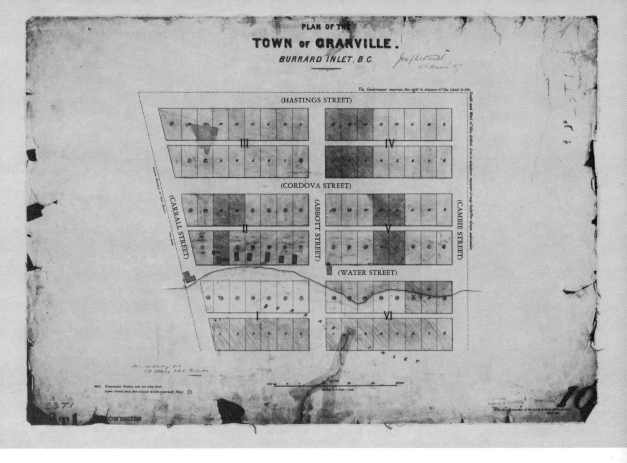

Present street names were not in the original plan, but have been inserted in brackets. The building standing on the road allowance at Carrall and Water Streets was Gassy Jack's original "Globe Saloon"; his second hotel, "Deighton House", stood on Lot No. 1 at the same corner. The crooked line roughly following Water Street is the original shoreline.

In 1866, John Thomas, nicknamed "Navvy Jack", started a rowboat ferry service from the hotel to Moodyville. In 1867, Navvy Jack was ousted; James Van Bramer brought his steamer *"Sea Foam"* round from the Fraser River and plied a triangular ferry route from the hotel to Moodyville and Hastings Mill (formerly Stamp's Mill).

The second and best-known owner of the hotel was Maximilian Michaud. "Maxie" had a good dance floor and a dance band. Soon after taking over the hotel in March, 1869, he opened the Inlet's first post office.

The population of Gastown was an explosive mixture of different races, nationalities and religions. Most people spoke Chinook, the trade jargon of the northwest coast; even court proceedings were often carried on in Chinook.

Sometimes the mill had to close for a couple of days after payday,

27

Granville, about 1884. Most of the buildings on the south side of Water Street faced directly on the Inlet; the few buildings on the north side of the street were set on piles, over the water.

Water Street at Abbott, Village of Granville, 1882.

because so many of the hands were gambling. Gassy Jack staged cock-fights for the South Sea Islander crewmen of the lumber ships.

There were sometimes a dozen deep-sea vessels in port at once. If several of the masters had wives aboard, entertainments, and even dances, would be held.

Education

In 1872, the Hastings Mill Company built a tiny wooden schoolhouse. At first, the school was operated privately by the mill; in 1873, with fifteen pupils, it became Granville School, under the Free Public School Act of 1872. The school had a wood stove, coal oil lamps, slates for the children to write on, and an organ for music. The teacher, Miss Georgia Sweney of Granville, was paid $40 a month.

Dim Prospects

Granville and Burrard Inlet seemed to have a precarious future. In 1866, the colonies of Vancouver Island and British Columbia had been united, with New Westminster as capital. But in 1868, the capital was transferred to Victoria. This meant removal of the Governor and his staff, and most of the civil servants, from New Westminster. The loss of prestige, population and trade was a severe setback, not only to New Westminster, but to the whole lower mainland.

The gold rush had collapsed and the lumber market — Burrard Inlet's main resource — was up one month, down the next. And what would happen to the area when its forest was cleared? Most of the land was no good for farming.

In 1871, British Columbia joined the Canadian Confederation, on the promise of a railroad to the Pacific, to be finished by 1881. One of the many routes proposed would reach the coast 130 miles further north at Bute Inlet, bridge Seymour Narrows, and run down Vancouver Island to Victoria. Under that plan, Burrard Inlet would remain just a hole in the coastline.

"A Wonderful Location"

In 1878, the federal government settled on a route down the Fraser Valley to the head of Burrard Inlet. Still, that would not do much good for the residents of Granville; they would sit in their village and watch the ships sail past, to and from Port Moody.

William Cornelius Van Horne, General Manager of the Canadian Pacific Railway, came from Port Moody to Granville, looked over the land, and said, "What a wonderful location for a seaport!"

Van Horne was echoing the idea expressed fifteen years earlier by Gassy Jack Deighton, who said, "... this inlet would make the nicest of harbours. It will be a port some day."

30

4
Growth Of
The City

By February, 1886, it was certain: the railroad was coming to Granville. Here was more deepwater harbour space than at Port Moody, and more space ashore for switchyards; here, too, ships would be spared the difficult passage through Second Narrows. As an inducement to establish the terminus there, the Provincial Government and private property owners granted the CPR thousands of acres of land in and around what was to become the new city.

New City, New Name

Clearing of the townsite began, and 125 Granville residents petitioned the Provincial Legislature for incorporation as a city, under a new name.

The name was Van Horne's choice. "This is destined to be a great city," he said, "perhaps the greatest in Canada. We must see to it that it has a name commensurate with its dignity and importance, and Vancouver it shall be, if I have the ultimate decision."

On April 6, 1886, Granville formally became the City of Vancouver; its boundaries followed approximately the present lines of Nanaimo Street, 16th Avenue and Alma Street.

The community's first newspaper had jumped the gun; on January 15, 1886, appeared the first issue of the *Vancouver Weekly Herald,* printed on a hand-press brought from Toronto.

On May 3, the men of Vancouver elected a Mayor and ten Aldermen. On May 10, Mayor M. A. Maclean, a real estate dealer recently arrived from Winnipeg, addressed the first Council meeting: "We commence

DRY GOODS & GROCERIES.   JAS. HARTNEY

Carrall Street
Copyright applied for

Vancouver, May, 1886, one month after incorporation as a city. The maple tree at the corner of Carrall and Water Streets served as a meeting-place and bulletin board.

The steps on extreme right led to Gassy Jack Deighton's second hotel.

today...to lay the foundation of a city which is destined...to take a prominent place among the most progressive cities of...Canada... Before many years pass, we will take our stand in the front for the Province of British Columbia, and second only to San Francisco on the Pacific Coast."

At the end of February, there had been only 100 habitable buildings in the village. By mid-May, the new city had 600, with many more under construction.

Even so, to outsiders, Mayor Maclean's predictions must have seemed absurdly inflated. In 1886, New Westminster had a population of 4,000, Victoria 14,000, Winnipeg 20,000, Toronto 118,000, Montreal 186,000, and San Francisco over 250,000. (Canada itself had 4.6 million.)

Soon after its election, City Council asked the Dominion Government for 1,000 acres of government reserve, between English Bay and Burrard Inlet, as a public park. Some citizens objected that the site was too far from town to be of any use. But two years later the reserve became Stanley Park.

Fire!

The morning of Sunday, June 13 was calm and hot. Slash-fires burned sluggishly at land-clearing operations.

About 2:30 p.m. a near-gale sprang up from the southwest, whipped up the fires, and sent flames racing towards the city.

There was no hope of fighting the fire, no equipment, no water; there was time only to grab a few belongings and run, or to jump into a boat and row.

The flames roared through the resinous Douglas fir of which the city was built. In forty-five minutes it was all over. Hastings Mill and a few other structures still stood, but nearly 1,000 buildings — few of them insured — were reduced to ashes.

The city had been crowded with strangers, so no one ever knew how many were burned alive. Of those who escaped, many lost everything they had.

That night, some took refuge in Moodyville and New Westminster; some slept, packed like sardines, in the few surviving buildings; some paced the bare, blackened streets.

Reconstruction

Vancouver was down, but not out. By Monday morning, tents were being pitched on the still-warm ground, and wagon-loads of lumber were rolling down the streets. Before sunset on Wednesday, a dozen firms were doing business in temporary shacks.

The morning after the fire, June 14, 1886, two months after incorporation as a city. The tent in the foreground stands at the southeast corner of Cordova and Carrall Streets.

The morning after the fire. Refugees' bivouac on the south side of False Creek, near the present intersection of Main Street and First Avenue.

Vancouver City Council after the fire, 1886.

Vancouver City Police Force, 1886, outside the temporary City Hall, after the fire.

July, 1886, five weeks after the fire: Cordova Street, looking west from Carrall.
For some years Cordova was the city's principal retail shopping street.

The Council, meeting in a tent, instructed the City Clerk to buy a fire engine and fire bell, and to have underground water tanks constructed for fire-fighting. A new bylaw required future buildings to be more solidly built. Brick and stone structures were soon being erected. Many buildings from this period still stand in the Gastown area. *See, for example, the Herman Block on the southwest corner of Carrall and Water Streets, the site of Gassy Jack's second hotel, Deighton House.*

By the end of 1886 there was a school, a hospital, a cemetery, an opera house, a bank, and a new two-storey City Hall. On Cordova, Water and Carrall Streets alone there were 14 office blocks, 23 hotels, 51 stores, 9 saloons, 2 stables, a church, a roller-skating rink, a mill and a wharf. At Coal Harbour the CPR was building a depot, a 1,000-foot wharf and three freight sheds.

In January, 1887, the Hudson's Bay Company opened for business on Cordova Street in a quaint building resembling a log chalet with gabled ends.

The city's water, drawn from wells, was sometimes none too clean. There were occasional outbreaks of typhoid fever, and citizens were pressing for water and sewage systems.

38

Hudson's Bay Company's first Vancouver store, Cordova Street, 1888: first opened for business in January, 1887.

The Terminal City

On July 4, 1886, the first scheduled transcontinental passenger train had reached Port Moody, 2,907 miles from Montreal.

By spring, 1887, the rails were extended to Vancouver. On May 23, 1887, the first transcontinental train steamed into the little wooden depot under the bluff, just west of Granville Street. Engine No. 374 was garlanded with flowers, evergreens, streamers and mottoes. On its headlight was a portrait of Queen Victoria — 1887 was her golden jubilee — and on its smokestack a sign, MONTREAL GREETS THE TERMINAL CITY. It hauled a baggage car, a colonist sleeper, a first-class car, a Pullman and a drawing-room car. *See Engine No. 374 in Kitsilano Park.*

The Fire Brigade paraded, the 6-piece Vancouver Band played, and more than 2,000 spectators cheered as dignitaries spoke of great things achieved, and still greater things lying ahead for Vancouver.

Arrival of the first scheduled transcontinental train at Vancouver, May 23, 1887.
The tender of Locomotive No. 374 is piled high with wood.

Trade with Asia

A week later, a CPR-chartered steamer *Abyssinia*, left Yokohama, Japan. On June 14 she docked at Vancouver with 102 passengers, 3 bags of letters, 11 packages of newspapers, and 2,830 tons of cargo, mostly tea.

A consignment of this tea was rushed by train via Montreal to New York, put on a fast steamship, and landed in London on June 29, twenty-nine days after leaving Japan!

The new trans-Pacific trade boomed. London to Yokohama via Vancouver was two weeks quicker than via Suez. The CPR secured a British Government contract to carry mail to Japan and China, and built its own ships; in 1891 the *Empress of India*, *Empress of China* and *Empress of Japan* began a mail, passenger and fast freight service that was to last for many years. *See the replica of the* Empress of Japan's *figurehead in Stanley Park.*

On May 16, 1888, the CPR opened its first Hotel Vancouver, away out of town at Granville and Georgia, to cater to passengers on the

Unloading tea from S.S. Parthia, Vancouver, 1887.

42

S.S. Parthia, Vancouver, 1887. One of three ships chartered by the CPR to carry passengers, mail and freight between Japan, China and Vancouver.

Arrival of the first CPR Empress ocean liner, RMS Empress of India, from the Orient, April 28, 1891.

trans-Pacific route. It had sixty rooms. Four people registered on opening day: Harold W. Topham and Edwin W. Topham of England, G. H. Hartnagel of Victoria and A. E. (Boney) Suckling of Vancouver, who probably registered on opening day for luck.

Boom and Bust

The early years were a time of growth and activity. Every boat and train brought new settlers. Land was being cleared rapidly and a street system laid out in rectangular blocks. Hundreds of houses were built in all parts of the city, generally costing from $800 to $10,000 each. Electric lights were installed, powered by a 50-volt generator.

Capilano River water reached the city by a pipeline under First Narrows; the incidence of typhoid was immediately reduced.

The first Granville Street Bridge was opened, a low-level wooden span, wide enough for two wagons to pass, and with a four-foot pedestrian sidewalk.

An electric streetcar system was started with six cars. One route went from First Avenue along Main, Powell, Carrall, Cordova, Cambie,

First Hotel Vancouver, southwest corner of Georgia and Granville Streets, 1888. In front of the building, on Georgia Street, are the hotel express wagon, for hauling baggage, and the hotel bus, for carrying guests to and from trains and steamers.

Hastings, and south on Granville to False Creek. The other went from Campbell Avenue along Powell, Carrall, Cordova, Cambie, Hastings, and south on Granville to Pender.

The Northern Pacific Railway, an American company, laid a branch line to Sumas, Washington, joining a CPR branch from Mission south to the border. Regular passenger and freight trains connected Vancouver with Seattle, Portland, San Francisco and the entire United States. An interurban tram service was established, with two trips a day between Vancouver and New Westminster.

Regular steamship services were established from Vancouver round Point Grey to New Westminster, and on up the Fraser River as far as ships could go. Routes also went to Victoria, Nanaimo and other B.C. coastal settlements, to Seattle, San Francisco and other American ports, and to Australia, with stops at Victoria, Honolulu and the Fiji Islands.

In June, 1890, there were five schools, with thirteen teachers and 1,024 pupils. The first high school opened with 31 pupils.

Vancouver, looking northwest from about Hastings and Dunlevy Streets, October, 1887, about one and a half years after incorporation as a city.

Picnic in Stanley Park, 1888.

Water Street, looking west from Carrall Street, about 1889. The building on the extreme left was still standing in 1974. Several buildings have balconies facing the street.

Hastings Street looking west from Cambie, 1896. Note the left-hand rule of the road, the two yoked oxen, the dog lying in the street, and the four-wheeled streetcar (fare, 5 cents).

Vancouver, 1895, looking north from the steeple of the first Holy Rosary Cathedral at Dunsmuir and Richards Streets. Upper right, old CPR station. The visible part of Granville Street is by now lined with stores and offices; Seymour south of Pender is mainly a residential street. Note the planked cross-walks at the intersection of unpaved Seymour and Pender Streets. The brick building at the northwest corner of Seymour and Hastings was still standing in 1974.

Cordova Street about 1898, still Vancouver's main shopping street. The streetcar conductor moves along the running board of open-sided car to collect fares. The building at left still stands (1974), occupied by Army & Navy Department Store.

48

In 1891, Vancouver's population reached 13,000. In 1892, South Vancouver was incorporated as a separate municipality. In the same year the first Woodward's Store was built at Westminster Avenue and Georgia Street. (Westminster Avenue was later renamed Main Street.)

In 1894, a cannon was set up at Brockton Point and fired daily at 6 p.m. to mark the fishing curfew. (It was eventually changed to 9 p.m.)

The arts and other leisure-time activities were by no means neglected. In December, 1887, the city's first library, the Vancouver Reading Room, opened above Thomas Dunn's hardware store at 136 Cordova Street. The following year, the bylaws of the Reading Room were amended to let women use it.

Three miles east of town, an oval race-track was cleared, close to Maxie's hotel; the new track was called East Park (now named Exhibition Park).

The new Governor General of Canada, Lord Stanley, visited Vancouver and on October 29, 1889, dedicated Stanley Park "to the use and enjoyment of people of all colours, creeds and customs for all time." *See the statue of Lord Stanley in Stanley Park.*

The newly-formed Vancouver Art Association, with forty members, held a loan exhibition in the Van Horne Block on Granville Street, including watercolours and oils by local artists, curios, a collection of fretwork, hand-painted china, and specimens of Indian arts and crafts. An amateur dramatic society was flourishing, and a Philharmonic Society was being organized. On December 5, 1889, the newly-opened Imperial Opera House staged the city's first Shakespearean production, Richard III.

Two years later the Vancouver Opera House opened next to the Hotel Vancouver on Granville Street with a performance of "Lohengrin", starring Emma Juch. For days previously, H. H. Layfield & Company at 16 Cordova Street had been advertising "opera colors in cashmeres, in silks; opera silk gloves, wool shawls, fans, opera hose, opera corsets (pink, blue, black) and opera kid gloves".

The city's first boom lasted only six years. By 1893, economic depression had settled over Canada, the United States and Europe. Vancouver, with its economy largely dependent on international trade, was hard hit. Unemployment was high; churches set up soup kitchens and daily fed hundreds of the destitute. Many railroads in the United States went broke; only its trans-Pacific trade kept the CPR going.

Race Relations

Until the early 1880s the native population on Burrard Inlet probably exceeded the white, and through the lumber industry and fishing the

Indians found a useful role in the white man's society. The two races got on fairly well together, and there was some intermarriage.

The railroad caused a huge increase in the white population, and a great development of commerce and industry; forest clearing rapidly changed the environment of the Inlet. Many of the newcomers were prejudiced against inter-racial marriages.

The white man had brought with him diseases against which the Indians had no immunity, and alcohol, a drug to which the Indians were not accustomed. The Indians' culture and way of life were disrupted; their population declined.

Indian women on a Vancouver wharf, 1901.

The 1891 Census of Canada classified the population of the New Westminster District, which included Vancouver, by birthplace:

Note: The Provincial boundaries have changed considerably since 1891.

British Columbia	14,102	Nova Scotia	1,134
United Kingdom	7,838	Manitoba	603
Ontario	7,429	Prince Edward Island	346
China	3,276	Newfoundland	215
United States	2,681	Northwest Territories	85
Quebec	1,460	Other countries	1,846
New Brunswick	1,169	Unknown	42
		Total	42,226

Outnumbered, and increasingly out of harmony with the booming white civilization, the Indians tended to withdraw from white society. Many of them abandoned their old homesites and moved permanently away from the Inlet.

The Golden Years

In 1897, came news of a fantastically rich gold-strike made the previous year in the Klondike. 1898 saw the unprecedented stampede of men, and a few women, from all over the world to the Yukon. West coast ports prospered. Vancouver merchants sold all kinds of useful and useless equipment to would-be prospectors; Vancouver hotels and lodging-houses had every bed rented, and men sleeping on the floors; jam-packed Vancouver ships carried men and supplies up-coast to Skagway, Alaska, jumping-off place for the Yukon.

By 1900, the Klondike boom was past its peak, but the influx of capital had triggered a period of rapid expansion. Immigrants poured into the city, and its population increased at a rate never equalled before or since, from 27,000 in 1901 to 100,000 in 1911, nearly quadrupling in ten years!

The newcomers were of many nationalities, but most were from Europe, Eastern Canada and the United States. The largest single bloc was from Britain.

Much of the prosperity stemmed from speculation in real estate; yet there was an underlying, real growth, based upon increasing development of B.C.'s natural resources, principally lumber, fish and minerals.

Local demand for lumber was expanding as the population of B.C. and the Prairies increased; and enormous quantities of lumber were

Loading Alberta grain for South Africa, about 1899.

shipped to Australia, South Africa, South America, the United Kingdom and China. The number and capacity of Vancouver's sawmills increased greatly, with many of the new mills being built on False Creek.

On April 18, 1906, earthquake and fire devastated San Francisco. That city, always a heavy buyer of fir lumber, absorbed 92.5 million feet in the process of rebuilding — double the amount it usually bought. Another earthquake at Valparaiso, Chile, in August of the same year, produced a further flood of orders. So great was the demand on coastal sawmills that there was a temporary shortage of lumber. Through the latter part of the decade, large cargoes of lumber were being shipped to Panama for use in construction of the canal.

Many fishing boats operating in the Strait of Georgia and up the west coast were based in Vancouver. During the 1880s and 1890s, numerous canneries had been established on the Fraser River and on the B.C. coast, and a huge trade in canned fish developed with the United Kingdom, Eastern Canada and Australia. Fresh fish, packed in ice, was sent by the CPR to Eastern Canada and Eastern United States.

The rich B.C. mining industry was now producing not only gold, but also copper, silver, lead and zinc, and Vancouver was becoming its financial and outfitting centre.

There was a great expansion of manufacturing; new plants were mainly located around Burrard Inlet and False Creek.

Vancouver's shipping traffic was increasing rapidly. The CPR put more ships on its runs to Yokohama and Hong Kong. New, larger steamers carried passengers to Victoria, Nanaimo and the Gulf Islands, and south to Seattle and San Francisco. Expanded steamer services carried passengers, mail and supplies up-coast to logging camps, mines and fish canneries, and to Alaska. New steamer routes were opened from Vancouver to Mexico, New York and New Zealand, and to the United Kingdom via the Suez Canal.

Increasing numbers of towboats pulled log-booms and barges to and from Vancouver.

In 1904, the Great Northern Railway (now the Burlington Northern) commenced operations on a direct route between Vancouver and Seattle, crossing the Fraser River by a new road-and-rail bridge at New Westminster, providing fast, economical service to the south and also, by its advertising, helping to make Vancouver better known in the United States.

Members of the Vancouver Bicycle Club at Prospect Point, about 1895. Note the absence of buildings on the North Shore.

Vancouver's first automobile, 1899, with gasoline-fired steam engine.

The following year, an electric interurban tram service opened to Steveston, over tracks that had previously been used by the CPR for steam trains.

In 1909, the second Granville Street Bridge, a high-level swing-span steel structure carrying streetcar tracks, was opened by the Governor General of Canada, Earl Grey.

In 1910, an electric railway line was built on the south side of the Fraser River, from Chilliwack to New Westminster, connecting with the existing tram-line to Vancouver. River steamers still carried bulky freight up and down the Fraser, but now, as the timberlands of the valley were cleared and cultivated, dairy products, fruits and vegetables were shipped to Vancouver by the electric railway company's daily "milk special".

Streetcar lines were extended until the cars were carrying 100,000 passengers a day; and by this time there were regular ferry services to West Vancouver and North Vancouver.

But people had other ways of transporting themselves. By 1900, the bicycle craze was in full swing. The automobile, as a practical means of

Hastings Street near Hamilton Street, about 1905.

transport, was still years off; many districts had no streetcar service; many families had neither space nor money for stables, horses and buggies. But nearly every home had one bicycle; many had two or more. Nearly all young men and women rode; so did some elderly men and even a few elderly women. There were big bicycle racks at City Hall, the CPR depot and the post office, at hotels and in the parks. On many of the busier streets, between the gutters and the wooden sidewalks, ran six-foot-wide cycle-paths, cinder-surfaced, rolled smooth, and regularly maintained by city workmen.

The first decade of the new century saw other major developments.

In 1906, David Spencer, a Victoria merchant of Welsh origin, opened a store in Vancouver. His Hastings Street business eventually became one of the city's major department stores.

In 1907, the Vancouver Stock Exchange was opened to replace the old mining exchange in regulating Vancouver's commercial interests in the hinterland.

By 1908, Shaughnessy Heights was being subdivided into residential lots by the CPR; Kitsilano was being built up; the city's best homes were in the West End. The portion of South Vancouver lying west of Cambie Street separated and formed the new municipality of Point Grey.

In 1909, the city's first skyscraper was finished, the 13-storey Dominion Trust Building at Hastings and Cambie (now called the Dominion Building). Many other tall buildings were under construction downtown.

In 1910, the first "Vancouver Exhibition", now called the Pacific National Exhibition, was held at Hastings Park, with an attendance of 68,000.

In 1911, Vancouver took in Hastings Townsite and District Lot 301, thus expanding eastward to its present limit at Boundary Road.

The harbour was being developed; the steam bucket-dredge *Mastodon* began its long task of widening and deepening First Narrows.

Vancouver had by now attained a dominant economic position on the west coast. It had superseded Victoria as the commercial centre of the province. New Westminster had seen itself outstripped in foreign trade and was coming to depend largely on the trade of the Fraser Valley.

The quality of life was changing. Vancouver had grown from a rough pioneer town to an elegant metropolis. There were dances, teas, receptions, picnics at Bowen Island, bathing-parties at the jam-packed beaches of English Bay. Automobiles became common and there was walking and driving in Stanley Park. The world's greatest performers — Charlie Chaplin, Sarah Bernhardt, Melba, Paderewski — appeared at the theatres and opera houses.

Hastings Street looking east from Granville, about 1907.

Charmer, leaving Vancouver, about 1905.

Granville Street, looking north from Georgia, about 1905. Centre, CPR station. The North Shore shows extensive clearing, but not many buildings.

Woodward's grocery department, 1904.

The beloved Joe Fortes at English Bay, about 1905. Joe, a Jamaican, came to
Vancouver as a seaman on the sailing ship Robert Kerr in 1885. Soon afterwards,
he appointed himself honorary lifeguard at English Bay bathing beach. He
rescued many swimmers in distress, taught many youngsters to swim, and made
himself loved by everyone. After his death, February 4, 1922, he received a civic
funeral. See the Fortes memorial in Alexandra Park.

The big tree, Stanley Park, about 1910. The automobile has oil and acetylene
lamps, no windshield.

English Bay, 1906. Right, the old bath-house.
Note that all men, except the one in the
bathing suit, wear hats; most women wear
hats and many carry umbrellas.

Digging the basement for an extension to the Hudson's Bay Company's store at Georgia and Seymour Streets with a steam shovel, 1911. The Birks Building, right centre, is almost finished.

Granville Street, 1914, looking south from the CPR station. Right foreground, old Post Office. Right centre, top, second Hotel Vancouver under construction. Note the many large buildings erected during the Golden Years.

The great boom was interrupted only by two short recessions, in 1904 and 1907. The year 1907 brought to a head the inter-racial hostility that had been simmering for fifty years. Back in the gold rush, many Chinese prospectors came to B.C.; then in the 1880s, several thousand Chinese labourers had been brought to B.C. to help build the CPR, and when that work was done, many of them settled in Vancouver. In the early 20th century, many of the immigrants were from Japan, China and India. Thus there was in the city a substantial minority of Asiatics, and some white people resented their competition in business and in the labour market.

The 1907 economic downturn caused considerable unemployment; the result was a heightening of this long-standing racial prejudice, and a series of clashes between whites and Orientals.

But the ill-feeling declined with the return of prosperity. Frantic speculation drove the price of land up and up until some lots in Vancouver were more expensive than in downtown New York!

People began wondering just how long the boom could last.

Depression and War

In September, 1912, the Governor General of Canada, H. R. H. The Duke of Connaught, son of Queen Victoria, opened the new Connaught Bridge, now called the Cambie Street Bridge. Yet amid the ceremonial and social glitter of the event, many Vancouverites were anxious: the land boom was over, and Vancouver was beginning to feel the effects of the oncoming world-wide economic depression.

Business activity slackened. Land values declined and many speculators were ruined. For example, a parcel of land at Cambie and Broadway, advertised at $90,000, later was sold for $8,000. The slump continued through 1913.

The Panama Canal was now nearing completion. There had been much debate as to the possible effects of the canal on Vancouver. Some people asserted that prairie products would still be shipped eastward by rail, as the quickest, cheapest route to the Atlantic and Europe. Others predicted a massive diversion of this traffic to Vancouver, thence by ship, via Panama, to the eastern seaboard of the United States, Africa and Europe.

Anyway, the harbour facilities were being enlarged. In 1914, the CPR built Pier D at the foot of Granville Street and the Federal Government built Lapointe Pier and a 1.3 million bushel grain elevator at the foot of Salsbury Drive. *See this grain elevator, which has since been expanded.*

On August 4, 1914, Canada declared war on Germany. On August 13,

A military parade at Granville and Georgia Streets, shortly after the outbreak of World War I, 1914.

Gun emplacements at Ferguson Point, Stanley Park, 1st World War.

the Panama Canal was opened, but it brought no immediate benefits to Vancouver. The war, with its heavy requirements for shipping of men and munitions, caused a world-wide disruption of normal seaborne traffic; German submarines and cruisers were harassing the sea-lanes. Naval guns were mounted in Stanley Park for harbour defence. The business of the port actually declined. Moreover, many men were leaving the city to volunteer for armed service. The depression in Vancouver continued throughout the first fifteen months of the war.

Towards the end of 1915 came an economic upturn. With completion of the Canadian Northern Pacific Railway (now the Canadian National) from Quebec through the Yellowhead Pass, Vancouver became the terminus of a second transcontinental railroad. To create land for switchyards and depots, the Canadian Northern Pacific and Great Northern Railways filled in one-third of False Creek, from Main Street east to Vernon Drive.

The increasing demands of munition factories raised the price of copper and B.C. mines greatly increased their output. The war cut off some European supplies of pulp, paper and lumber, and B.C. mills helped meet the demand. Ships were urgently needed to make good the Allies' losses; so B.C.'s shipbuilding industry emerged from the doldrums.

In 1916, the second Hotel Vancouver was completed at Granville and Georgia Streets.

Silt dredged from False Creek was being used to build Granville Island; the project was completed in 1917.

Peace and Plenty

On November 11, 1918, World War I ended. Vancouver's boom continued.

World shipping traffic increased, and now Vancouver began to feel the effects of the Panama Canal. New markets opened for B.C. lumber in Eastern United States. Vancouver merchants could now import products direct from Europe and supply not only B.C. but also the Prairies more cheaply than their competitors in Toronto and Montreal. Vancouver's traffic continued all winter, while eastern ports were icebound.

The second Hotel Vancouver, completed in 1916 at Granville and Georgia Streets.

Vancouver was becoming an important wholesaling and trans-shipping centre. The fruit jobbers of Water Street bought and sold peaches, plums, pears and apples from the Okanagan. Vancouver plants processed milk, cream and cheese from the dairy farms of the lower Fraser Valley. To Vancouver stockyards came the beef cattle of the Cariboo.

New industries were started, old ones expanded. Factories were built on Granville Island.

The downtown area was changing rapidly. Small stores and houses gave place to massive commercial buildings, opulently decorated.

Prosperity brought a great increase of population, and a keen demand for housing. New subdivisions sprang up. East and southeast, along Hastings and Kingsway into Burnaby, and south into South Vancouver, were mainly working-class homes. West, along Broadway and up on to Point Grey, were streets of middle-class homes. South, along the inter-urban railway tracks to Kerrisdale and down the south slope, truck gardens tended by Sikhs and Chinese were replaced by the big, garden-set homes of the well-to-do.

The 1920s brought major developments in the arts and entertainment. In 1920, the B.C. Art League was formed, and started a campaign for the establishment of an arts and crafts school and a permanent art gallery in Vancouver. In 1922, radio broadcasting began in Vancouver on station CJCE, but few people had radio receivers. The most popular public entertainment of this decade was vaudeville. Its chief home was the old Orpheum Theatre on Granville until, in 1927, the New Orpheum opened two blocks farther south on the same street. The centre of stage and screen entertainment was moving from Hastings to Granville.

On January 1, 1922, Vancouver discarded a bit of its British heritage when traffic was changed from the left to the right side of the street. The doors of all the streetcars had to be converted to let passengers board from the right.

In 1925, a bridge across the Second Narrows linked Vancouver, by road and rail, with the North Shore, formerly accessible only by ferry.

A great expansion of the sawmilling industry was beginning; many new mills were located along the North Arm of the Fraser River in the municipalities of Point Grey and South Vancouver.

The prosperity of the 1920s permitted the realization of a long-dormant plan. In 1899, Vancouver High School at Dunsmuir and Cambie Streets had become Vancouver High School and College, affiliated with McGill University, Montreal. The first college class had six students. Seven years later the College was renamed McGill University College of B.C.

70

The new campus of the University of B.C., at Point Grey, October, 1925.

In 1912, the College moved to temporary shacks on the grounds of Vancouver General Hospital. In 1915, it closed and the University of B.C. officially opened, using the facilities, staff and students of McGill College. The government allotted the western portion of Point Grey as a permanent site for a university, but years passed and no move was made. At last, with the boom, there was money for higher education; in September, 1925, the students abandoned the General Hospital grounds and began classes in new buildings at the Point Grey campus.

By the end of 1928, the city could look back on thirteen years' uninterrupted growth. In 1921, 496 commercial deepsea ships visited the port; in 1928, 1,344. The mid-twenties saw the end of regular use of sailing ships. Regular bulk grain exports did not begin until 1921; by 1924 they totalled 53 million bushels; by 1929, 95 million. The total cargo shipped through the port was:

| 1921 | 3.2 million tons | 1928 | 9.9 million tons |

West and North Vancouver ferries
at the foot of Columbia Street,
Vancouver, about 1928.

False Creek, looking east from Granville Street Bridge, September, 1928.

Vancouver waterfront, 1927.
Foreground, foot of Granville Street.

English Bay, 1928. Note the large number of people swimming and on the diving rafts.

Granville Street, looking north from Robson, 1925. Birks' clock is visible at Granville and Georgia. The old Hudson's Bay Company store advertises "June Bride Week". Top left is the second Hotel Vancouver.

76

Hastings Street, looking west from Cambie, 1927.

Siwash Rock, Stanley Park, October, 1927.

78

The Great Depression

The year 1929 began with a celebration. On January 1, Vancouver absorbed the municipalities of South Vancouver and Point Grey, increased its area from 16.5 square miles to 43.7 square miles, its population from 149,000 to 228,000 and became the third largest city in Canada. The Greater Vancouver area now had about 300,000 people.

The boom rolled on. For the past two years speculators had turned from real estate to stocks, and were doing better than ever. It was said that there were over eighty millionaires in the city.

Then, in October, 1929, the stock market crashed.

Vancouver was hard-hit. Building came almost to a standstill. Local and American lumber sales shrank; sawmills went on short time, or closed. Wheat shipments declined. By December, bread-lines were forming outside the City Relief Office.

Vancouver had more than enough of its own citizens out of work.

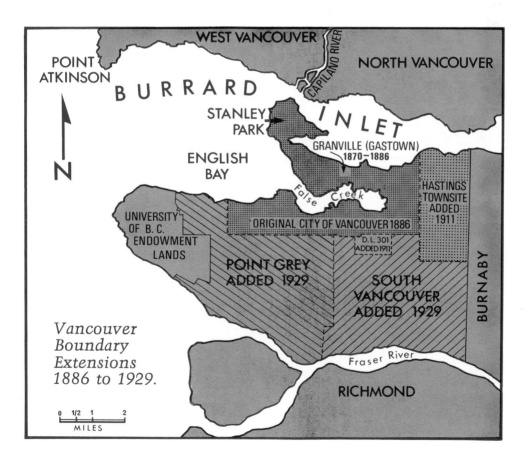

Vancouver Boundary Extensions 1886 to 1929.

But to the city came thousands more unemployed, from shut-down mines, logging camps and fish canneries. Many more came from other provinces; if they could not find work, they could at least escape the prairie winter.

The year 1932 saw the completion of the Burrard Bridge and unemployment for many of the men who had worked on it.

By the winter of 1932-33, nearly 40,000 men, women and children — about 15% of the city's population — were living on relief or unemployment benefits.

At the annual tax sale in November, 1933, 2,481 lots were put on the block; only 125 were sold, and 2,356 fell to the city.

In December, 1933, the city's schools were about to be closed for lack of funds. To keep them open, the teachers agreed to work the month without pay. In the end, they did get $24.24 for the month! Teachers earning less than $1,200 a year accepted salary cuts of 10%; those earning more took 20% cuts.

In November, 1934, 3,700 parcels of property, including nearly 1,000 homes, were up for tax sale, but there was almost no one willing to bid on them. So on November 12, City Council passed a bylaw cancelling the tax sale for that year, and allowing six years' grace for payment of back taxes.

There was no national unemployment insurance scheme. Family men without jobs received scanty benefits jointly funded by city, provincial and federal governments, and were allowed to stay at home. Single unemployed men, to get relief, had to go to road construction camps far from the cities; they put in eight hours a day and got food, work clothes, shelter, and twenty cents a day spending money.

In April, 1935, 2,000 men left the relief camps and marched to Vancouver, demanding "work and wages". They invaded the Hudson's Bay Store, clashed with police, and then marched to Victory Square for a mass meeting. Mayor Gerry McGeer read the Riot Act, ordering the crowd to disperse. Opposition to the Mayor's action culminated in a 24-hour sympathy strike by many local workers, and a meeting of 15,000 people urging abolition of the so-called "slave compounds".

By the end of 1935, Vancouver was on the verge of bankruptcy. In that year the city's share of relief costs was $1,200,000 in a total budget of $14,200,000; tax arrears had reached $8,300,000.

Actually, the worst of the depression was over. A slight economic upturn had begun in 1934, and Vancouver saw some signs of it.

The new City Hall at 12th and Cambie was finished in 1936, at a cost of $1 million. That year was the city's golden jubilee. To mark the oc-

*Hastings and Cambie Streets: unmarried, unemployed
demonstrators during the Hungry Thirties.*

casion a fountain with coloured lights was built in Lost Lagoon; many taxpayers called it a waste of public funds.

Sea Island airport had opened in 1931; in 1937 it attained international status with commencement of flights to Honolulu.

Lions Gate Bridge, built to facilitate development of a great new residential area, British Pacific Properties, at West Vancouver, was completed in 1938.

But there was still much unemployment. In 1938, 1,500 demonstrators, demanding a public works programme, seized the Art Gallery, Hotel Georgia and the main Post Office at Granville and Hastings. At the Post Office and Art Gallery they held out for a month, until ousted by police with tear gas.

In 1939, the new Hotel Vancouver, at Georgia and Burrard, opened, at that time the tallest building in the city. The old Hotel Vancouver at Granville and Georgia was closed, and its contents sold by auction.

Figures for total cargo shipments through Vancouver show how far the "hungry thirties" had slipped below the "roaring twenties".

1928	9.9 million tons	1934	6.3 million tons
1929	9.6 million tons	1935	6.3 million tons
1930	7.0 million tons	1936	7.8 million tons
1931	7.3 million tons	1937	6.9 million tons
1932	7.2 million tons	1938	6.4 million tons
1933	6.1 million tons	1939	7.0 million tons

Partly-finished Lions Gate Bridge,
June 15, 1938. Empress of Russia
is entering the narrows.

King George VI and Queen Elizabeth on Granville Street, 1939.

Downtown Vancouver and part of the West End, 1935. Left, the
Marine Building; centre, the new Hotel Vancouver, not
yet finished; right, the second Hotel Vancouver.

World War II

As in 1914, the outbreak of war in September, 1939, brought no immediate boom to Vancouver. Coastal defence guns were set up. The federal government took over the old Hotel Vancouver, first as a recruiting centre and later as a barracks for soldiers and headquarters of the army's Pacific Command.

Leaving for the internment camps, 1942.

But for most Vancouver people, life changed little until the bombing of Pearl Harbour by the Japanese in December, 1941. A blackout was at once imposed. Thousands of citizens of Japanese origin were hustled off to internment camps in the interior of B.C.

After the initial panic subsided, the blackout was changed to a less inconvenient "brown-out". By federal government order, the city's water supply was chlorinated for the first time, despite public protest. Ottawa felt the step was necessary to protect the health of military and naval personnel.

In 1941 began an influx of men and women from the central and eastern provinces, seeking work in Vancouver's expanding shipyards, aircraft and munition factories. At the peak of production Vancouver and Victoria shipyards employed more than 30,000. Thousands more worked at the Boeing Aircraft plants on Sea Island and at Coal Harbour and False Creek in Vancouver. The population of the city reached 275,000, that of Greater Vancouver 400,000.

Despite this prosperity, shipping traffic was hard hit by the war. Total shipments slumped even below the slack years of the depression.

1940	6.5 million tons	1943	5.6 million tons
1941	6.4 million tons	1944	6.8 million tons
1942	5.8 million tons	1945	7.0 million tons

Postwar Development

After the war's end in 1945, population increase and wartime scarcities of labour and materials left the city with a housing shortage. In January, 1946, the year of Vancouver's diamond jubilee, a group of returned veterans and their families — 700 in all — invaded the empty old Hotel Vancouver at Granville and Georgia. They remained there as squatters for awhile, then had their occupancy approved, and the building served as a veterans' hostel until its demolition in 1949.

It had been bought in 1948 by the T. Eaton Company, which planned to build a store on the site; but in the same year Eaton's bought the business of David Spencer Ltd. at Hastings and Richards. The old hotel site was levelled and used as a parking lot. (It was not until 1973 that the T. Eaton Company opened its new department store on the site.)

Many servicemen who had seen wartime duty on the west coast returned here with their families; tens of thousands of immigrants came from war-torn Europe. Vancouver's population grew rapidly: in 1941 it had been 275,000; by 1951 the city had 345,000, and Greater Vancouver 588,000.

Hastings Street, 1952, looking west from Seymour Street. Right foreground, a one-man streetcar; right centre, the old Post Office; left centre, the Marine Building.

Industry and Commerce

The early 1950s began a period of rapid economic growth. Capital poured in from Eastern Canada, the United States and Europe; old industries expanded and new ones were started. Shipping traffic increased; after more than twenty years, cargo movements through the port began to exceed those of the 1920s.

1946	8.2 million tons	1956	13.4 million tons
1947	9.0 million tons	1957	13.1 million tons
1948	9.0 million tons	1958	11.6 million tons
1949	9.4 million tons	1959	11.4 million tons
1950	10.1 million tons	1960	12.4 million tons
1951	11.2 million tons	1961	14.0 million tons
1952	12.1 million tons	1962	14.6 million tons
1953	11.8 million tons	1963	16.9 million tons
1954	11.5 million tons	1964	19.8 million tons
1955	11.0 million tons	1965	20.2 million tons

Centennial Pier and Ballantyne Pier, Vancouver, 1971, with ten freighters moored.

In 1966, the National Harbours Board extended the official boundaries of the Port of Vancouver from the 49 square miles within Burrard Inlet to nearly 200 square miles, reaching to the United States border. First Narrows was being deepened to fifty feet, but for many of the new bulk carriers this was still too shallow. The new bulk-loading facilities at Roberts Bank in the Municipality of Delta had a minimum depth of sixty-five feet; the 50-acre site, at the end of a 3-mile causeway, opened in 1970 to export coal from the Crowsnest Pass area to Japan.

Trade with the Pacific Rim countries became increasingly important for Canada and Vancouver. The annual value of this trade, excluding the Americas, increased from $583 million in 1960 to $3,328 million in 1972.

Mainly as a result of the increasing bulk traffic, cargo tonnage movements began a rapid rise.

1966	21.7 million tons	1970	27.2 million tons
1967	23.1 million tons	1971	35.3 million tons
1968	24.2 million tons	1972	36.7 million tons
1969	23.1 million tons	1973	42.1 million tons

Pollution

For some sixty-five years the residents and industries of Vancouver had, without much thought, increasingly befouled the air and the sea around them. *See the photograph of False Creek pollution on page 72.* At length they attempted to reverse the trend.

During the 1950s the railroads replaced their smoky steam locomotives with diesel-powered units. Pipelines brought oil from Alberta (1953) and natural gas from the Peace River District (1957) to the coast; thousands of domestic and industrial furnaces that formerly burned coal, wood and sawdust were converted to the new fuels.

During the 1960s most of the local sawmills stopped burning their waste in beehive burners and began selling it to pulpmills. New government regulations forced industries to reduce their smoke output.

The result — the air became clearer all over the city, buildings cleaner, and winter fogs fewer and thinner.

Yet there was a rapid increase of air pollution from another source — less visible than the coal and wood smoke, but not less harmful. By 1970, about 75% of air pollution in the Greater Vancouver area was from automobile exhausts. Estimated annual amounts at that time were 479,000 tons of carbon monoxide, 87,000 tons of hydrocarbons, 20,000 tons of nitrogen oxides, and other pollutants in smaller quantities. A B.C. government study in 1972 showed pollution from this source high enough, at times, to damage vegetation and human health.

The first major step in reducing water pollution was to stop the long-established practice of dumping raw sewage into the sea. In 1963, much of it was diverted through the Highbury Tunnel, four miles long, nine and one-half feet in diameter, running from Jericho under the Burrard Peninsula and the North Arm of the Fraser River to a new primary treatment plant on Iona Island, between Sea Island and Point Grey.

Yet in the water, as in the air, while one source of pollution was being curbed, another was developing. There were in the early 1970s several oil spills from ships, befouling the beaches and threatening the marine life of the Vancouver area.

Transportation and Communications

Beginning a few years after World War II, major transportation changes were to alter the appearance, the commerce, the whole life of the city.

The colourful but noisy streetcars were replaced by the quieter trolley buses: the last streetcar was withdrawn in 1955.

In 1956, the Pacific Great Eastern Railway (now the British Columbia Railway), was extended from Squamish via Horseshoe Bay to North Vancouver, and connected by the Second Narrows Bridge with the CNR,

CPR and GNR. This gave Vancouver, for the first time, a direct north-ward route to the interior of B.C.

Better communications — movement of all first-class mail by air (1948), completion of the Trans-Canada Highway (1962) and development of jet planes — speeded the flow of information, businessmen and tourists to and from Eastern Canada and the United States and facilitated business operations here.

The ferry service from Vancouver to West Vancouver, started in 1909, ended in 1947. Ferry service to North Vancouver had begun in 1866 with Navvy Jack's rowboat, and developed to a fast, frequent service with large vessels carrying vehicles and foot passengers. This service ended in 1958. People preferred to drive over the First or Second Narrows Bridges rather than ride the boats.

On January 22, 1974, six blocks of Granville Street between Hastings and Nelson were closed for the construction of a permanent pedestrian area with two lanes for bus traffic only.

The City and the Suburbs

Rapid population growth in the post-war years produced major changes in the city's appearance. First in the West End, later in other areas, single-family houses were demolished and replaced by apartments — at first two and three storey wooden buildings, later by concrete high-rise towers.

Yet the city could not accommodate the hundreds of thousands of people coming to live in this corner of Canada. The result was a relatively slow growth of the city and fast growth of the suburbs.

Date	Greater Vancouver	City	Suburbs
1951	588,000	345,000 (59%)	243,000 (41%)
1961	828,000	384,000 (46%)	444,000 (54%)
1971	1,082,000	426,000 (39%)	656,000 (61%)

The suburbs include the University Endowment Area, the City and District of North Vancouver, West Vancouver, Richmond, Delta, Surrey, White Rock, New Westminster, Burnaby, Lions Bay, Port Moody, Coquitlam, Port Coquitlam, Maple Ridge, Pitt Meadows, the City and District of Langley, Indian Reserves and unorganized areas in Greater Vancouver.

Suburban housing developments, formerly all single-family subdivisions have, in the 1960s and 1970s, come to include a mixture of low and high-rise apartments.

Extensive bridge and highway construction has helped to speed suburban growth by facilitating travel to and from the city. Among

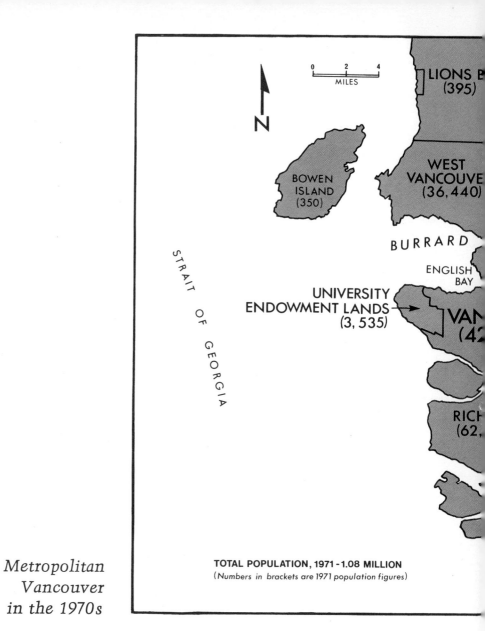

LIONS B
(395)

WEST
VANCOUVE
(36,440)

BOWEN
ISLAND
(350)

BURRARD

ENGLISH
BAY

STRAIT OF GEORGIA

UNIVERSITY
ENDOWMENT LANDS →
(3,535)

VAI
(42

RICH
(62,

TOTAL POPULATION, 1971 - 1.08 MILLION
(*Numbers in brackets are 1971 population figures*)

Metropolitan
Vancouver
in the 1970s

the most important projects leading south are the new Granville Street Bridge, 1954; Oak Street Bridge, 1957; Deas Island Tunnel, 1959 (later named George Massey Tunnel); Vancouver-Blaine Freeway, 1962, through Richmond, Delta and Surrey to the United States border; and Knight Street Bridge, 1974. Leading to the east are the Port Mann Bridge and the Trans-Canada Highway, through Burnaby, Coquitlam, Surrey and Langley, both opened in 1964. The new Second Narrows Bridge, completed in 1960, improved access to the North Shore.

Lack of space in Vancouver forced most new industries to locate in the suburbs; for the same reason, many old established industries, wishing to expand, had to move to the suburbs.

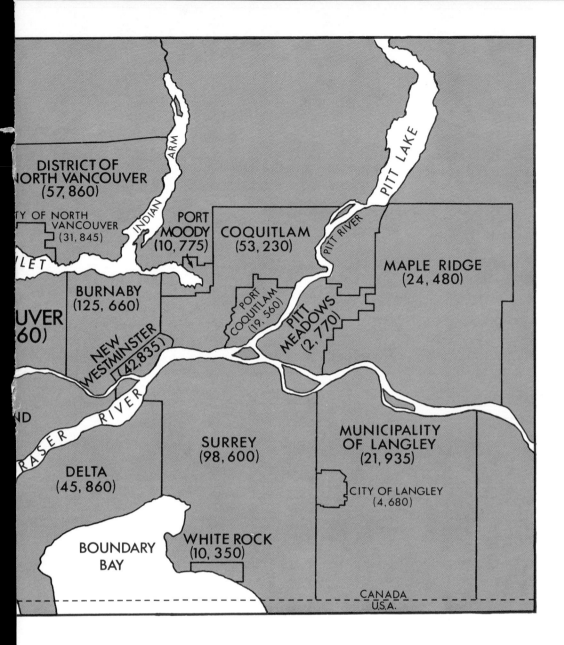

DISTRICT OF
NORTH VANCOUVER
(57,860)

Y OF NORTH
VANCOUVER
(31,845)

PORT
MOODY
(10,775)

COQUITLAM
(53,230)

MAPLE RIDGE
(24,480)

INDIAN ARM

PITT LAKE

PITT RIVER

LET

BURNABY
(125,660)

UVER
60)

NEW
WESTMINSTER
(42,835)

PORT
COQUITLAM
(19,560)

PITT
MEADOWS
(2,770)

ND

RASER RIVER

SURREY
(98,600)

MUNICIPALITY
OF LANGLEY
(21,935)

DELTA
(45,860)

CITY OF LANGLEY
(4,680)

BOUNDARY
BAY

WHITE ROCK
(10,350)

CANADA
U.S.A.

By 1974, most of the industries were gone from the shores of False Creek; the land was being developed for housing, marinas, waterfront walkways and public parks.

The City and the Province

In 1971, 50% of B.C.'s population lived in Greater Vancouver. Vancouver had become the distribution centre of the province, the main source of labour, the major port, the financial, commercial and cultural centre.

It is often the first and only part of B.C. that many visitors see. In 1973, there were 201 conventions in Greater Vancouver with more than 100,000 delegates.

Sports and Pastimes

Soon after World War II there began a rapid expansion of facilities for sports and entertainment, which continued right through into the 1970s.

In 1948, the first television programme reached Vancouver from Seattle. It was not until 1953 that the CBC began local television broadcasting.

1949:   The first chair-lift was built on Grouse Mountain, to the 2,900

The West End and Downtown Vancouver, 1972.
Top left, part of the Port of Vancouver.
92

foot level; in 1951 the second chair-lift was added to 3,600 feet; in 1966 the Gondola was constructed to this same level.

1954: The Empire Stadium was built on the Pacific National Exhibition grounds. It has been used by the B.C. Lions football team, and for other athletic activities.

1956: The aquarium opened next to the Stanley Park Zoo.

1959: The Maritime Museum opened in Kitsilano Park; its chief exhibit is the RCMP vessel *St. Roch.* In the same year the Queen Elizabeth Theatre opened; the Playhouse was added in 1962.

1963: The Sea Festival started, featuring a street parade, salmon barbecue, fireworks over English Bay, and displays of Indian canoeing, dancing and handicrafts.

1968: The H. R. MacMillan Planetarium and Centennial Museum were opened near the Maritime Museum, just west of the site of the old Indian village, Snauq.

1969: Theatre in the Park began outdoor musical comedy performances in Malkin Bowl, Stanley Park (similar to those produced from 1940 to 1963 by Theatre Under The Stars). In the same year, the Bloedel Conservatory opened on Little Mountain in Queen Elizabeth Park, offering displays of tropical plants, trees and birds under a triodetic dome.

1971: The completion of the First Narrows section of Stanley Park seawall opened an all-seasons walk right around the park shoreline.

In the early 1970s there was a sudden revival of interest in cycling; bicycle Sundays were held in Stanley Park; a new cycle track was opened exclusively for bikes, about half-way around the park.

History Comes to Life

Vancouver people have become more interested in their city's history.

The old Gastown area has been revitalized, with stores, art galleries, restaurants and night clubs. In 1970, a statue of Gassy Jack Deighton was erected in Maple Tree Square, at the intersection of Carrall and Water Streets. On September 30, 1972, at New Westminster, Mayor Muni Evers unveiled a headstone on the grave where Gassy Jack had lain, unmarked, for ninety-seven years.

Also in 1972, the City of Vancouver Archives opened in Vanier Park, next to the Centennial Museum and Planetarium. The building was dedicated to the late Major J. S. Matthews, Vancouver's eminent archivist.

In 1974, Vancouver Mayor Art Phillips led a campaign to buy the Orpheum Theatre, built in 1927, and to restore it as a second major live theatre for the city.

INDEX

INDEX (cont'd)

SOURCES OF INFORMATION

We hope that this book will arouse in some readers the desire to find for themselves more information on various aspects of Vancouver's history that especially appeal to them. From our experience in gathering material for this book, we can recommend the following sources:

GENERAL INFORMATION ON
VANCOUVER'S HISTORY
Vancouver Archives
Provincial Archives, Victoria
Vancouver Public Library
*Special Collections division of the University
    of B.C. Library*
British Museum, London, England
SHIPS
Vancouver Maritime Museum
MAPS
Vancouver Archives
Provincial Archives, Victoria
Vancouver Public Library
*Special Collections division and Map division
    of the University of B.C. Library*

PHOTOGRAPHS
*Photographic division of the Vancouver Public
    Library*
Vancouver Archives
Provincial Archives, Victoria
Vancouver Maritime Museum
*Notman Photographic Archives,
    McCord Museum, Montreal, Quebec*
*National Portrait Gallery,
    London, England*

OLD NEWSPAPERS AND MAGAZINES
Vancouver Public Library
Vancouver Archives
Provincial Archives, Victoria
University of B.C. Library

ABOUT THE AUTHORS

RAYMOND HULL

Raymond Hull is a best-selling author, an internationally-known lecturer and a broadcaster. He has lived in British Columbia since 1947.

Some of his recent books: *How To Get What You Want; Profitable Playwriting; Writing For Money In Canada; Tales Of A Pioneer Surveyor; The Peter Principle* (with Dr. Laurence J. Peter); *The Art Of Making Wine* and *The Art Of Making Beer* (with Stanley F. Anderson); *Home Book of Smoke — Cooking Meat, Fish and Game* (with Jack Sleight); *Gastown's Gassy Jack* (with Olga Ruskin).

He has had thirty TV and stage plays produced and five stage plays published.

Raymond Hull has worked on the Yukon River sternwheel steamer *Casca* and on the B.C. coastal steamer *Camosun.*

GORDON SOULES

Gordon Soules is president of the consulting firm Gordon Soules Economic and Marketing Research.

Since 1961 he has gained much knowledge about Vancouver's past from conducting economic and marketing research studies on many aspects of the city's development. He is author of numerous research reports, and of the books *What People Want In A Library* and *Vancouver At Your Feet.*

CHRISTINE SOULES

Christine Soules is a Vancouver social worker. She obtained a degree in Politics and Economics and a Diploma in Social Work at Keele University, England. In 1966 she came to Vancouver and in 1969 obtained her Master of Social Work degree at the University of B.C.

Books published by GORDON SOULES ECONOMIC and MARKETING RESEARCH
VANCOUVER'S PAST, Raymond Hull, Gordon Soules and Christine Soules
VANCOUVER AT YOUR FEET, Gordon Soules
GASTOWN'S GASSY JACK, Raymond Hull and Olga Ruskin
WHAT PEOPLE WANT IN A LIBRARY (A technical book for librarians), Gordon Soules